AF435188

ALSO BY NATE McCALLUM

The Universe He Carried

Heartbreak + Healing

Half a Life / Half a Lie

Losing Grip

If I Stay Silent

SYMBIOSIS

OF

HEART & SOUL

ECLIPSED EDITION

POETRY COLLECTION #5

BY: NATE McCALLUM

Where Symbiosis Starts

to my family, my friends, and time
thank you for being patient and finding a piece of life
I now call mine
a heart once shattered, now mended anew
for that, I dedicate this book to you

to my parents who never gave up on me
who held my hand and helped me see
life is a journey with ups and downs
with love and support, we can turn things around

to my sister, who always has my back
who never let me fall through life's cracks
for your love and laughter fulfills this life
and I am grateful to forever have you in sight

to my friends: Gabbie, Wyatt, and Chris
who stuck by my side through the highs and the lows
who offered a listening ear and a helping hand
reminding me I'm not alone in this land

to the world that slowly healed my heart
and helped me find a brand-new start
the hibiscus has bloomed after the rain
the light has followed through the pain

I dedicate this book with love and grace
to those who helped me find my place
for without you, I wouldn't be here
grateful and confident with nothing more to fear

A Note from Nate

Over five frivolous years have come five fretful books containing the stories of my life. Since releasing my first book, *"The Universe He Carried"*, in 2018 I have found poetry as a guiding force in my life as a means for my self-expression, self-reflection, and betterment of my health. So much of my poetry has been enlaced in my shame, denial, pain, and heartache, however, never were stories revolving around the beauty surrounding my life consistent. *"Symbiosis of Heart & Soul"* is a love letter and celebration of my monumental fifth poetry collection to highlight that even the dark thoughts can be lessons learned with hope still standing. It's the stories that extend over the course of a year in growing and learning what it means to be human once again. *"Symbiosis of Heart & Soul – Eclipsed Edition"* is the complete picture of the healing I underwent and includes twenty poems originally meant for the initial release that I decided to reserve for their subject matter. However, one year later I can sit back and understand these are poems that add much more perspective to my life. What once belonged to me, now belongs for the world to see.

Now sit back, take a deep breath, and prepare for a deep dive into the stories that have shaped the individual I am and am still becoming. It's time to experience what it means to have my very own symbiosis eclipse.

-    Nate McCallum

The Stories

PART I – *The Divergence*................
Stories of defeat and denial

Intro to Divergence
Unraveled
Bitter End
Dance Floor Glasses
To the Boy with Blue Eyes
Mutual
The Price of Love
Venti White Mocha, No Whip
Muffled Voices, Muffled Choices
Autumnal Mortem
Dreams of the Defeated
The Bluebird's Song
Factory Reset
Without the One I Know
Fickle and Fragile
When Is It My Turn?
Coiling Pt. I
Silent Sentiments
Around the Bend
Lost Cause
The Pawn
Silence
22
Static
The Monster
Spiral
Trophy Boyfriend
Blue Lights
Could I Capture It?
Proving Her Wrong
Don't Take My Childhood Away
Holy
What's Wanted Isn't Always Granted

PART II – *The Projection*...............
Stories of anguish and adjuration

Intro to Projection
Villainization
Puppy-Eyed Boy
Hellish Haven
How Could You?
Heartbreak Anthems
Abysmally Blue
Hung Up
Whispers of Ruin
The Reign of Darkness
Empty Promises
Cusp of November
Skin & Bone
Love of the Cruel Kind
Forsaken Felony
Karma
Devotees
Dismembered
Winless Game
Asinine Apologies
Fixation
Bones of the Unbound

PART III – *The Alignment*...............
Stories of reflection and realization

Inro to Alignment
Sacred
Architect
In a Dream
Return to Chapter One
Every Little Misstep
Nightly Rendezvous
Remain Red

Coiling Pt. II
Clear
Garden of Growing Up
Velvet
24 Hours
Surrender
Lavender
Be Patient with Me
Wait for My Heart to Decide
To My Grandparents
Lavender
Will the World Still Turn?
Cursory Connections
Rewind
Three-of-a-Kind
High Tide
Repair the Rope
Not the Same
588 Days
Borderline
Weathered Boots
End Goal
Summer Symphony
Dissertation of Escapism

PART IV – *The Symbiosis*...............
Stories of synergy and self-growth

Intro to Symbiosis
Symbiosis of Heart & Soul
This is Love
Memories Traced
Wishing Well
The Boy with the Guitar
The Best Sides
Euphoric Dreams
Strength of a Father
Eyes of a Mother
Happy New Year

Ex Deposition
Little Things
Colors Pt. III
Hibiscus
Compass of Campus
Gabbie
Wyatt
Chris
Tethered Threads
Tapestry of Life
Fruits of Forgiveness
First Fall of Snow
Pages of the Past
A Brother's Love
Where Hope is Fed
The Life I Choose
Reclaimed
Eclipsed
The Universe I Carried

PART I
THE DIVERGENCE

Intro to Divergence

in search of harmony, the heart and soul unite
striving to synchronize and shine bright
a quest to discover my true purpose and role
to find symbiosis that can make me whole
with each step forward, a new horizon appears
as the journey unfolds, the path will become clear
the heart and soul beat in unison and rhyme
guiding the way to a life that's sublime
though alignment may come, and projection may
block
the heart and soul persist, never to be knocked
for the bond is unbreakable, and their purpose divine
to find symbiosis and a life that's fully aligned

Unraveled

unraveled identity
can't recognize the one in front of me
heart heated from the hurt
soul buried deep within the dirt
jealousy and jaded friends
ongoing cycle that never ends
insecurities infiltrate each time,
isn't this supposed to be my prime?

drink away the ingrained thoughts
what's a few more shots?
highs, lows, and despair follow after
miss who I was and the once sincere laughter
symbiosis of heart and soul
whom I'm becoming I still don't know

each mistake piles into oblivion
a finish line I can no longer win
dead reputation can't be revived
at least I'll know I survived
to lose yourself is to lose sight
clinging to what's left of me with might
pray it doesn't all succumb to the darkness
I'm just waiting for my light

Bitter End

who have I become?
is it someone better?
or a manifestation
of the worst part of me?
this can't be true
these things I now do
used to the appeasing
but where am I now?
anything but myself I'm feeling
hold my breath
and count to ten
maybe I'll learn to love myself again
once I push through this bitter end

Dance Floor Glasses

not sure how I ended up here
not sure if I'll make it clear
one too many drinks in my system
caught feelings and kissed him
glasses found on a wet dance floor
a souvenir of a night I'll forever store
give my all to a night with no recollection
to a broken heart longing for affection
pray nobody sees me at this moment
pray these dance floor glasses can hide this love-
strained lament

So Much More

I don't need the minds of the forgotten
to determine my value
they'll never see me beyond the surface
and all I'm destined to do
this life is fragile
and wears at each figment of what I should be
brush away the yearning for acceptance
when I'm content just being me

but what would you know?
I am so much more
I am a brother,
I am a lover,
I am a follower,
I am a creator

beyond the judgments of the fray
I am the sum of my dreams living each day
I am not defined by others' sight
but by my fire within burning bright

To the Boy with Blue Eyes

chasing time, but this time I'll take it slow
the race of the chase is all I've ever known
keep my heart close and see how it goes

to find who should be the one
and have it end before all is said and done
took my heart and held it with a gun

so foolish to fantasize it could be true
to assume I was ready for someone new
so foolish to fall for the boy with blue eyes
when the love you led on was only a disguise

Mutual

hold a head high with a slight smile
keep strong at least for a little while
won't show the cracks in my heart
what I've been feeling since we've been apart
was the release truly mutual
when the timing was so unusual
tell our friends it was cordial
but I've been feeling anything but normal
how long must I fake this heartbreak
hours pondering on a feeling I can't shake
regret projecting my hurt onto you
wish there was a better way to get through
regret putting my heart on the line
thinking I got it right this time
regret taking one too many drinks
say my peace, and watch as your heart sinks
all these things I now must live through
but I never regret falling in love with you
so I'll continue to keep my lips sealed
my sadness guarded with an iron shield
I hope "mutual" is enough for you
but I'm still left thinking
what did I do to have my heart again broken in two

The Price of Love

affliction of a heart in solemn undertones
thought I waited my entire life for you
but then again, that's how love often goes

my hope lost in the span of twenty minutes
sweet talk in my ears to feed temporary pleasure
if that's the price of love, I'll take what I can get

was any of it real?
what was growing suddenly gets knocked down
right when I began to not just immerse
but finally feel

in the end, it's always wasted time
taking the memories and making them rhyme
cherish the beauty even when it's brief
learning the price of love is silent grief

Venti White Mocha, No Whip

though I'm with somebody new
I fear I'll never get over you
for if the rain were to pour in my direction
I'd splash back without discretion
how these days now lay bittersweet
when it's your eyes I no longer get to meet
never foresaw falling in love again
but to find someone special I allowed my soul to
bend
take the memories and hold them in my heart
allow you to remain with me forever
and with someone new, I've created a new start

Muffled Voices, Muffled Choices

indescribable bliss lasts mere hours
each second reminding me of what once was ours
a subtle glance to the side
continue dancing with hands held tied
in a room of muffled voices
I remain left with muffled choices
did I ever tell you how nice it was to see you smile?
missed the opportunity, but made a night worthwhile
each goodbye always comes back to haunt
when it's you I still seem to want
part ways yet another time
into new lives longing for that once-bright shine
moving on has never been this painful
when loving you remains so shameful
yet another night
where I hold onto the moment with all might
awaiting the so common cycle
of revisiting a love once seen as bible

Autumnal Mortem

a step in crisp air sends signals to this heart
earth decaying to once again restart
walk familiar paths that you had once shown
same trees placed next to old cobblestone
and the reflection of a once-sacred lake
shows new ways of how to reawake
touch the stones we once used to sit
a slight breeze passes as teeth would grit
they say time will work its unseen magic
but sometimes these days feel static
useless experiences when not shared with you
useless endeavors we'll never see through
how I've changed since last January
but to say, "I'm doing ok", would be the contrary
to look upon memories and for once smile
tears cascade from a time worthwhile
happy to have what I once did
moving on slowly, yet memories never feel candid
sometimes when I spot you in a crowd
I give a light grin and hope you're proud
to share so much of my life with you
now lead different lives but share the same view
so may the rain wash the scars
and let the memories remain the stars
for this life will carry on
with what we had forever remaining ours

Dreams of the Defeated

unexpected encounters when I least need them
not sure why I still reciprocate when I end up numb
shouldn't have ditched my friends
and lose sight of my heart once again
they're playing my favorite song in this club
but your familiar eyes remain my holdup
could capture this moment for hours
after the alcohol sinks something sours
"I did it to myself", so I told my mom
late-night tears with no hope of staying calm
to wish and dream endlessly of your face
when I should be praying for space
to stay up until I see the sun slowly rise
staring at a wall, but wishing it was your hazel eyes
to want something with my entire heart
for it to occur and find myself once again falling apart
dreams I believe should remain a memory
because seeing you now in this reality
won't equate to the fantasy
that you'll one day come back to me

The Bluebird's Song

simplicity in its purest form
sends healed hearts
to weather another storm

time remains frozen in birdcages of ivy
only existent in dreams
when love becomes a vivid reality

may the bluebirds sing another song
let time take its toll
to the broken hearts rewriting their wrongs
may the locks be broken
of the cage holding this love burden

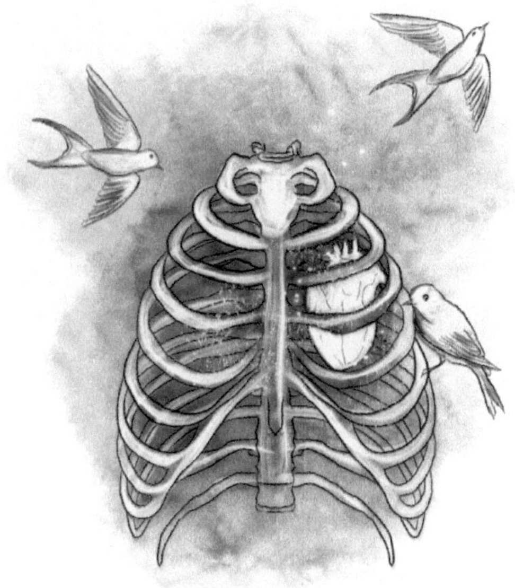

Factory Reset

each time you once again walk away
I clench my heart in disarray
though still a steady pulse, it beats in pain
what's been lost I pray finds a way to regain

wishful thinking for a full factory reset
erase the memories of love and regret
cleanse my heart of the scars you've left behind
free my soul from the bond that binds

longing for a fresh start and a new dawn
where the souvenirs of our love are finally gone
step into the arms of a new face
without the shadows of our past to chase

as you walk away, I release my grip
hope for healing from this heartache's grip
may time be the antidote to soothe and mend
a future that has an end
without the remnants of the one
who has since been long gone

Without the One I Know

I don't know who to talk to
not sure what to hold in my hands
where do I point my eyes to view?
because nobody else understands

how do I go on with life
without the one who knew
the parts of me that are true
nobody in this life can comprehend
the extent of our love that I still defend

first fall of snow without the one I know
guess that's how life goes
without the comfort of your nectar
I'm no longer a lover
but your protector
shield our memories with tears
for the rest of my life even when we had 2 years
ground frosts and this house is getting cold
where are you with willowy arms to hold?
where are you to soothe my labored breath?
where's the man who said he'd be there until death?

not sure which direction I'm supposed to go
but I'll figure it out
without the one I know

Fickle and Fragile

I once believed love to be true
inspired by stars and the friends I knew
a love that lasts forever strong
a bond that lasts our whole lives long

but now I see it all in vain
love is a fickle and fleeting game
a fragile flame that eventually burns out
leaving us lost and consumed with doubt

the stars whose love I used to crave
suddenly shattered by life's torrential wave
and friends whose love seemed pure and real
now torn apart by the lies they concealed

tried to find something of substance
found it once, and let it go with reluctance
all the songs of love have grown old
for if love is real
I'm no longer certain my story will ever be told

When Is It My Turn?

it's been two long years since love was found
each night I wander lost and unbound
the memories of what love once was
become the pain of love's lost cause

I long to feel the warmth of a heart
to feel the rush that comes from a new start
but love seems to be out of reach
a lesson they never seem to teach

the saying begins to burn
"when is it my turn?"
the feeling that I've been left behind
while others find love, I begin to resign
late nights alone and blue
wondering if love will ever find a way to renew

Coiling Pt. I

at which degree must a burn run too deep
when I bend, break, then let the ash seep
those I once found to be eternal
are the ones I leave thoughts internal
"delusional" or "disoriented"
when all I called for was a friend to lift my head
stuck in a simulation of whom I've become
pull a performance to reject the past of living as none
deservedly knowing there's so much more
than constant contradiction left in store
but would you care
to hear me out without a judgmental glare

Silent Sentiments

in silence remains echoes of regret
slowly churning, unwilling to forget
and to hurt one more person
is to fall back into a place before it can worsen
on the outside where I belong
play one more memory, one more song
and to find myself at once having everyone
lost trust, lost faith, returned to none
hearing, "There's no sign of change"
realize love of any remains out of range
and sometimes I wonder,
would my emotions ripple the ocean
when my actions are taken as a fraction
of a soul trying to find its end goal

Around the Bend

the future looms in a darkened cloud
fear that strikes with screams so loud
the demons lurk around every bend
fear that's hard to comprehend

I want to stay in these youthful ways
where life is an exploration with carefree days
the outside world remains a daunting thought
demons approach and cannot be fought

fear regression of all I've gained
facing the world with all its new pains
progress made can quickly fade
due to life's reality and all its cynical ways

Lost Cause

I am a lost cause
beyond the reach of friends
a ship adrift in stormy seas
a journey that never ends

they try to throw me lifelines
to guide me back to shore
but I am consumed in this darkness
and can't be found once more

my friends, though they care so deeply
and it hurts them to see
the state I am in
the person I have come to be

but I am a lost cause
and they cannot save me now
no matter how hard they try
the depths of my mind won't allow

so I drift into the ocean
a lost and lonely soul
fading into the darkness
where the broken hearts take hold

but in my heart I still love them
and cherish all they've done
for trying to save the lost cause
in a battle that could never be won

The Pawn

web of lies in a blood-soaked blanket
this infidelity was a sinister gambit
innocence exuding from the pawn I used to break
free
all because this love wasn't meant for me

if desperation was my destiny
I'd have chosen peace instead of deceit
tangled in the threads of my design
sought escape, regardless of the line

fueled by fear with an unwillingness to sever
played the part of both deceiver and believer
in the end, nobody was let off freely
from the chains of the lover that was never meant to
be

regret weighs heavy in the most cynical of my deeds
I wish I'd chosen a path where I planted gentler seeds
won't ever release the weight of what I'd done
a betrayal of trust in a battle never won

there were kinder paths I could've tread
but to tarnish his humanity was not worth all the tears
he shed

Silence

when one mistakes silence as a betrayal
they misinterpret the core of one's portrayal
take enough time to find the realization
process my own dictation
a life being held in constant castration
lost grip and repaired the rope
stayed silent and lost all hope
have matured and won't fight my mind
leave the others who bind me in their confines
thoughts that remain sacred to me
are not ones to be discussed freely
leave it for me and my poetry
give it a day, week, or month
ensure what I portray is not just a front
if my silence is sensed as sorrow
if my silence is not enough thorough
then silent I shall remain
until I once again heal my brain
and leave behind those who grave immediate change
instead of me once again being sane

22

well wishes from familiar faces
celebrations in traditional places
the world at once wrapped around you
now that twenty-one has turned twenty-two
twenty-four hours set to remind
that one day in three hundred sixty-five is aligned

keep tabs on those who reach out
those who don't cast doubt
check the phone each passing minute
wait for the lost loves to send something illicit

tomorrow the shimmer of life will resort
to one struggling to be traversed
into a familiar cold bed
where each tear is shed
though just another year
one day in which life finally feels clear
reinforcement of those caring for what you do
even after all these years
even after turning twenty-two

Static

few days of thoughts
lead to mind-struck chaos
few nights of bad dreams
figuring out what the value of life means

which target do I shoot the blame on next
until I realize
it's myself I've always been against

monotony gets so mundane
after staring at the same ceiling
day after day

now I'm listening to songs my ex used to sing
something about winter
nostalgic nights and waiting for my phone to ring

a sip of coffee in late November
lost a few friends
pray the good memories they'll remember

invite a boy over who I've been seeing
he's unlike any before
first time in years my heart is not fleeing

call my friend to bicker over boy problems
"I've been there once too,
just wait until your heart fully blossoms".

but what's the worth if these days stay stagnant
gain a little and lose a lot
waking up feeling but a fragment
of the life I led suddenly going static

The Monster

is the wicked monster the world portrays
truly worthy of all the words they say?
is a monster truly vicious with ill-intentioned fangs?
or the easiest medium in which projection hangs

when dusk rises do the misunderstood lurk to kill?
or is it the idea that keeps others still?
around these streets, all that's heard is,
"Don't fall for any trick of his"

into hiding, into silence, into the confines of
forgiveness
if the wicked goes missing, is there any good left to
reminisce
misguided times wrapped in a misguided life
living through another day, vicariously through their
strife

Spiral

sometimes when the drinks become too strong
I wait around the club waiting for you to come
prove I'm doing better or at least act like it
a smile on my face before the voices attack

shouldn't miss what was mine when it was hell
it was friendship even if my reputation they now sell
and you looked at me tonight with a smile
unsure if it was mockery or genuine
will accept either so long as I don't spiral

Trophy Boyfriend

the coffee cup once kept on the bedside counter
thrown away just as the memories of the first
encounter
always bragged that an ex talked highly of me
claim me as your own and then set me free
was I simply a trophy to be won?
was I naïve in believing when you said, "You're the
one"?
nights of saying, "You're the love of my life"
if two weeks is a life, then it's not a life well-lived
breathing through the scars of my skin
exhale and forgive me for letting this ever begin
if I have to give all of me one more time
I'll wait for a man who doesn't reassure "You're all
mine"
to get back at an ex to further diminish his shine

Blue Lights

sat down putting on my best face
for a love I'll soon erase
used to the scenarios when sweetness sours
at least I'll have the memories that'll stay ours

empty bottle of wine ends with cries in empty stalls
a friend to catch the tear as it falls
fix my hair, wipe my face, and turn a smile
into a night where it'll be worthwhile

few more drinks and clutch my chain
anything to numb whatever remains of pain
new faces appear and my lips abide
freedom feels good when it remains on my side

forgot the feeling of individualism
these blue lights are tonight's escapism
night ends next to someone new
how quickly life continues even without you

never pictured this as the start of a new year
numbness with painted-on tears
for why value the rose when the garden awaits
away from what was short-lived
hoping I'll end up in the right place

Could I Capture It?

could I capture the memories of March?
the freshness of friends
the souvenirs we now rewatch
text messages we'd constantly send

could I capture the memories of May?
never lover and new outlooks
they're tarnishing, but won't seem to stray
even with his dismal it now looks

could I capture the memories of June?
days of laughter and nights of pride
the crossroads of life approaching soon
just when I was about to hit my stride

and the memories of September
show I should've captured it all sooner
because all I seem to remember
are the memories remaining lunar
out of reach, but forever with me
love turns to hostility
wish I could've captured it
when there was still a grain left of my humanity

Proving Her Wrong

my mother's words continue to haunt my soul,
"you'll never make it, you're just a fool"
with every step I take in life
I feel her doubts cut like a knife
her words pressurized with a heavy weight
crushing me down with their cruel fate
trying to rise, but continuing to fall
if this is what I get, refuse to pick up the call
I feel like giving up and in
when I'm just waiting for my life to begin
deep inside I know she's wrong
won't let her doubts dictate my song
so I will rise and try again
even if it all seems in vain
I know deep down inside
my dreams cannot be denied
and though my mother may not see
there's a potential that's living within me
I will strive to prove her wrong
show her what it means to come out strong
I'll push forward with all my might
and rise above and show her my concealed light

Don't Take My Childhood Away

the world stops and I feel my heart thump
news hits midday and my throat catches a lump
mother messages as she says, "Grandma's in the
hospital"
a working boy stops as she instills
stay strong and hold onto hope
don't think in defeat, think on the scope
but it's 3 am and I don't have it in me to sleep
projections of potential pains continue to creep

turn the light on and for the first time I begin to pray
please don't take my childhood away
please allow my grandma to stay
let her be the fighter I've always known just one more
day

Holy

holy is the heart that beats slowly
divine remains a future approaching closely
fire igniting within my eyes
burn away the ashes of a long-run disguise
will Hell neglect the sins I've accounted?
will Heaven remain with faces surrounded?
never been one of religion
but, who's to amend my decisions
my body a temple of misfortune
my actions surpassed the margin
forgiveness in who I've been
is to forgive the fibers of my entire skin
hold the weight of my past
into a future I ensure will last
will the infliction ever be forgiven
for forgiveness never easily given
fall to my knees and say one more prayer
that my past won't forever impair
a soul that isn't too far gone to spare

What's Wanted Isn't Always Granted

I want something more than what life offers
hold my breath when the dreams seize
would try to express how I'm feeling
but would rather not be a bother

these days are slipping by
and I have nothing to show for my age
if I go to my tomb now
tell those in the future I truly tried

once thought I could cling to the rope I forged
but cut the strings and back down I return
this isn't how it was supposed to be
scar tissue that was sealed somehow becomes gorged

friends send reassurance and try to call
this silence is more comforting
me, the splits on my skin, and the ceiling
and god, please save me before I once again fall

this isn't what I wished my life to be
I wanted to touch the skies and uproot the trees
I wanted the love that would be of stories
I wanted the little things and all their glories
I wanted pride from my friends and family
all these wishes are vanishing from my hands
it's drifting just as the wind takes the sands
this is never how it was supposed to unfold
pray this life of mine has a spark of fuel left
before my story remains one fully untold

PART II

THE PROJECTION

Intro to Projection

no longer defeated, no longer sad
my anger burns hot like wildfire, I'm mad
others' words may try to bring me down
but refuse to let them take my crown
heartbreak from once trusted hands
left me shattered and unable to stand
but now I stand tall, find strength to be unbreakable
fueled by the fire of the unshakable
I won't let the pathetic dim my light
or tell me I'm wrong when I know I'm right
I'll rise above, fueled by this rage
and show the world my true power and sage

Villainization

in a world of angels and the wicked
remains a contest of who will become the villain
designed to leach on the vulnerable
eyeing those who are soon to fall
no sudden movements
or it'll be your final moments
life is a game of chess
finding ways to make one regress
idolize the misguided
and leave their insecurities subsided

the wicked of the world
never noticed, hardly observed
their good conscious can't redeem their sour heart
bad intentions are never at fault
but the reputation of the underdog
are left with an end with no epilogue
stories silenced by deafening dialogue
but there remains hope amongst the doubts
within the hesitance, beyond the shouts
with the love for those who believe
there's no limit left unachieved

Puppy-Eyed Boy

does your false narrative of resentment
fulfill your savior complex sentiments?
two months of tight-lipped thoughts
and two months later it's you who plots
preying on the gold of my heart to shift blue
pounce at the chance a narrative fits your point of view

abused a heart not healed
while I stood lips sealed
compare me to the ones before
take a body count of five or more
to paint me as the whore
took the scars on a wrist
and distort my pain as your blacklist
five months later, and still, I remain pissed
gave the world, the sky, the stars
and was left with silent scars

maybe you'll never care
but karma comes to those who dare
I still pray God leaves your life to spare
for I've given up on each and every swear
on a boy who never grew a pair

remain oblivious to your hatred
knowing you took advantage of something sacred
carry on with life acting the hero
but without my love, you would remain a zero
and you'll prevail as the puppy-eyed boy
who took my vulnerability as your very own play toy

Hellish Haven

how much of myself must I bend
until I'm enough to be the one you hit send?
can't you see I'm no longer happy?
skipped a few meals, and god I'm hungry
was even losing thirty
worth getting your attention to be flirty?
a brand-new outfit bought
praying your fixation is finally caught
do everything, more, and beyond
dyed my hair because you prefer them blonde
a face full of scruff now shaven
hope my heart isn't still too far graven
for a man who will never be my haven

How Could You?

told, "You don't need to worry,"
yet deceit slips through your lips so slick
your lies unfurl when you glimpse at me and hurry
you're inhumane and someone sick

how could you?
your falsehoods spread like fire
each promise shattered in a liar's choir
your deception leaving me in despair
but I rise from your treason now aware

is it jealousy or inevitability?
seeing your treachery laid bare
never trust a man's capability
if you think he won't, just know he'll dare

so tell me now
as you revel in your sin
how could you?
and where does your guilt begin?

Heartbreak Anthems

tear-soaked shirt as you stand in front of me
knew in a second it wasn't meant to be
so quickly love sours
sweet remedies can't save what was ours
where does love go?
where it quickly vanishes, I'll never know
were the highs even worth my time
knowing you never wanted to be mine
lie through your teeth for three fatal months
all I gave was never going to be enough
what we once so gently called love
has turned into a look away and a shove
thought I finally got it right
escaped the darkness and found my light
solemnly I'll hold onto the time we shared
and lament that you never even cared
I've grown tired of heartbreak anthems
when my happiness is held at ransom
so one more time I'll write off the woes
for the love of myself
is the only one I'll forever know

Abysmally Blue

right where I expected you to be
making an entire fool out of me
ludicrous to cry over you this late
when I finally found you in checkmate
so delicate we once used to speak
but those whispers have turned into screams
can't fathom how you can't say hello
when you were the one that let me go
a juxtaposition of where I once was
live long enough to see what karma does
took my blame, you took the high horse
standing tall with not an ounce of remorse
grown too old for these elementary antics
putting my belief in the hopeless romantics
so onward I'll continue
into a search for love
that won't leave me abysmally blue
into a search for love
that reminds me nothing of you

Hung Up

sprawled out in bed watching rain creep down a window
social media the genocide of progress
when witnessing my past move on sends me to a new low

I'm sure my ex says sweet nothings of our love
but it was real to me
even when fighting for it was shove after shove

barricading the actuality in one-sided remarks
but do they know the sacrifices made
when it was the two of us during the cusp of dark?

watch brown hair turn to blonde
how the roles change, but it looks good on you
tried to say it, but you didn't respond

and now my old friends celebrate his birthday
I hope they're having fun
assurance nothing I said ever had a say

maybe I'll see some friends to calm the confusion
why am I concerned
over a love who never cared what my value is?
it's been six months later from a one-month fling
so how is it that I feel the need to cling
to a mortified future led on an invisible string?

Whispers of Ruin

tribulations of how months change a routine
silence of souls of a new reality obscene
rumors run ramped in late night hours
something sweet somehow shifts sour
to live, learn, and lose
over whispers, I did not choose
is there room to grow on death row?
would change ever be enough to show?
a hurt heart screams with a vengeance
was shutting me out always the intention?

The Reign of Darkness

darkness reigns in a heavy shroud
a weight that's hard to lift in a steady crowd
the light seems so far away
a distant hope that never stays

trying to find a way out
break the darkness with a shout
seems to swallow me whole
and takes away my very soul

see a glimmer in the night
a ray of hope in its guiding light
it's fleeting and suddenly gone
and remain left with another day to carry on

this darkness lingers in my mind
a place where light is hard to find
each time I try to break free
the darkness finds ways to consume me

feel the weight upon my hollow chest
a heavy burden that won't let me rest
trying to find the strength within
fight the darkness and one day win

Empty Promises

if a heartbeat stops slowly
just know I think of you only
a picture of you from friends
will the torment ever end?
how could I ever move on
from the one I once forever called the one
look in crowded rooms
praying for a glimpse of you
each day prolonging the future
each new face painting a new picture
missing you more than I can say
holding onto the memories each day
I love you and remain unsure if I can stop
when moving on has remained the hardest part
given up when I still believe in us
as dusk falls, each pillow absorbs each cuss
just hope you're doing ok
and if I could see you for one more day
know that I'll never again stray

Cusp of November

the air feels different when one isn't living the same
a night out with a few too many drinks
left early from the same ongoing shame
but would you even care?

and everyone was circling without a glance
shy away, holding hands, and pointed posts
the words left unsaid are the actions that attack
and maybe I deserve this…

gained a few fake friends and now they're leaving
say, "We're here for you now"
God save the souls who keep on believing
but hey, I'll give it a chance

was so close to slipping and saying, "I love you"
hold my tongue and catch my breath
fear you'll never truly feel the same as I do
if you want the truth

return to an empty bed on a night that never ends
late nights and could use a friend
suddenly crying to the one on which my heart
depends
she who has seen it all

may the morning rain rinse the hangover
head held high amongst the storms
holes of my heart will soon patch over
the death of a heart that was buried on the cusp of
November

Skin & Bone

I am more than just my skin and bone
but that's all people seem to hone
focus on my body with judgmental stares
as if my worth is only found there

I wish they'd see the person within
the one that's kind, but has a dose of sin
the one that laughs, loves, and cries
not just the one pleasing to the eyes

why can't they see the thoughts I have
or the passions that make me glad
why can't they see the love I give
the way I curate my life and truly live

I am more than just my body and form
I am an external heart that has been reborn
I am a person with feelings and a soul
so why is my worth only defined by my role

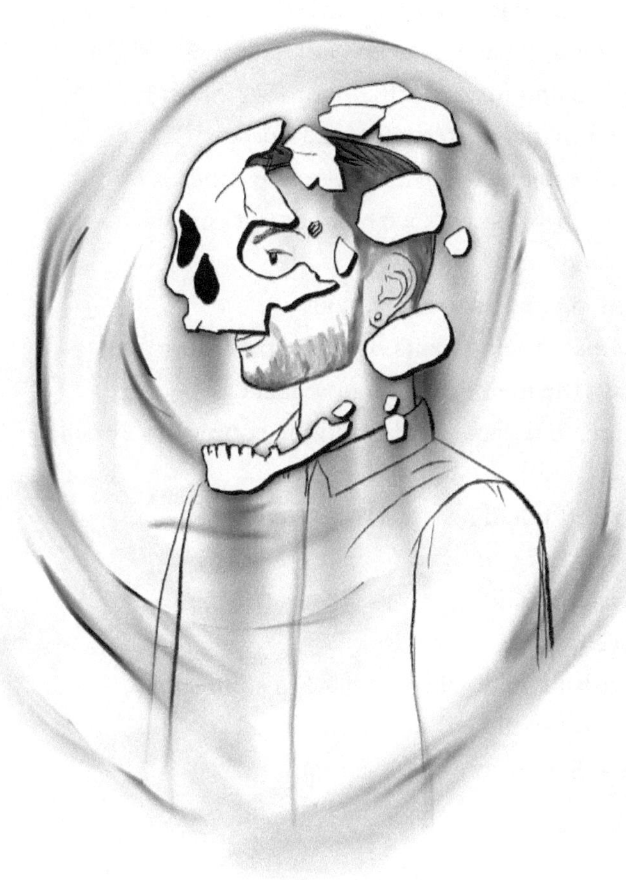

Love of the Cruel Kind

how cruel love always plays
when missing you is an endless game
searching for a specific photo
of a memory only you and I know
replaying videos where we once dance
and the moments we had our last chance

the piece I have left of you
remain the figments of what you used to do
and the memories you now make
remain dreams until I find the courage to awake

wish I could text you
see what you're up to
wish I could call you
see what you now do
wish I could tell you what I'm still feeling
wish I could say one more time,
I still love you

Forsaken Felony

freshness turns to falling turns to failing
the petals of a pure heart continue straining
another lost cause of a forbidden future
if this was destined, why couldn't it have happened
sooner?

left my heart on the porch of your parents' house
curled into bed left with ongoing doubts
but I remember…
the barren apple orchard in late October
picking you out a sweater in my favorite color
telling me, "You're unlike any other"
boast to friends of me taking something sacred
see the road of ruin you now lead of what I created
guess we never could share the same sight
that a three-week fling
would shift to memories of the night

Karma

I hope that karma bites back hard
at those who wronged me from the start
for every lie and every deceit
may they suffer a fate just as bleak

actions left a bitter taste
a life of lies unable to erase
hope their guilt consumes them whole
let them feel the pain they caused to unfold

may karma catch up and do its part
to punish them for each broken heart
for every tear shed and every fear
may they feel it all, crystal clear

I won't hold back, saying it straight
karma is coming just like fate
for every wrong they thought got away
may it come back to them, and make them pay

Devotees

those who found unity in isolation
brought together the burdened
to be left as the first burned
but without my belief, you would never be
took a chance and set myself free
prioritize my mistakes before your own
a month later, couldn't care that I'd grown
what a fool I must forever live with
thinking this would be different
an outsider only has a heart until there's power
when I bestowed it, you left me to cower
the icy reputation that clung to an ex's name
a newly single boy drowning in his shame
and the once-best friend who falls for their painful
game
but, without my goodwill
there would never be
the group of outsiders turned cynical devotees

Dismembered

provoked night out to prove a point
twist my leg and dislocate the joint
mocking my sentiments in half-assed jokes
feast on my peace to keep an ego stroked
six months and still on your mind
seek pleasure through crossing the line
choke the jugular until you spot spit
doesn't this methodical madness seem pathetic?
cut me loose for you already dug the grave
for a reputation that shouldn't have to be saved

Winless Game

whatever may linger has been cursed to kill
rob me of my sanity
now robbing me of my free will

distort half-truths to please your guilt
what happened to friendship?
the rose garden I tended has begun to wilt

months of recovery and still seek to attack
thought I found safe land
but you're taking me right back

to the nights of shame
playing a winless game
make claims I'm some racist
when the reasons remain baseless
paint me in an evil light
holding my heart with might
moved on, so why can't you
jealousy is jaded, but this isn't the person I knew
cynical endeavors tied with cynical motivations
regardless of where, forever held in your castration

won't let the words of the pathetic
rile me to being overdramatic
won't let the lies
send me to another night of cries
praying that one day you'll remember
the love we had for one another
instead of painting me as the villain
for the social battle you risked your morality to win

Asinine Apologies

six months have passed since you said those words
obscenities that cut like a thousand swords
my reputation was in ruin, shattered and torn
by your anger, hate, and venom you sworn

and now you come back with an apology in tow
but it's too late to make things right, that much you should
know
I had to bear the brunt of your rage and spite
and now you expect me to forgive without a fight?

the wounds you left were deep and raw
healing took time, effort, and more
left me to pick up the pieces
while you went on enjoying all of life's breezes

asking to forgive you and offer me a second chance
hoping I'll forget and resume our once blissful dance
it's too late now to make amends
the damage is already done, and I've found better friends

I'll always remember the good times we shared
even now, I hope you know how much I cared
what you did was vicious and surpassed what I inflicted
but is the friend you knew for a whole year *truly* worth the
image you depicted?

Fixation

in the hours approaching midnight, I feel your stares
persist
like hawks circling, the judgment insists
half a year has gone by, yet you hold some grudge
eyes like daggers, whispers an unwanted nudge

I've moved on and let go of the pain
but you cling to bitterness through your heart's
disdain
I no longer seek confrontation or strife
I yearn for a peaceful and harmonious life
yet you choose to linger with eyes locked on me
why can't you just set me free?

why must anger still consume your soul?
is it because my life now is no longer in your control?
I beg for you to move on and find your way
to seek joy through other ventures each day

shouldn't have to write this, but I say it with
conviction
I won't be the target of your endless affliction
I deserve happiness away from the weekly glares
to live my life freely, without constant despair

Bones of the Unbound

how much blood will strain from a body that doesn't
belong to me
they're chewing on the bones of a corpse that can't be
seen
ivy surrounded and sins unbounded
continue rotting in a body that can't be accounted
flesh peeling and muscle showing
it's pruning from the inferno of pressure growing
watch the flies feast on fecal flesh
this life was supposed to end in gentle rest
watch a beautiful being turn into fragments
a life with such promise has become static
gave up too much to fulfill their desires
life gets lost when one puts out too many fires
pray the rebirth is one to achieve an unfulfilled
promise
for the void in this life was waiting to grow into a
goddess

PART III
THE ALIGNMENT

Intro to Alignment

from anger and projection, I've found a way
to use the past as fuel for each new day
learned to see the beauty in pain
and use it as a means to grow and gain
no longer dwell on what's been done
instead, focus on what I've become
with every step, I find peace and light
and see the world with new and clearer sight
to be happy, I've learned, is not to hide
or simply hope that good things will arrive
it's to embrace both dark and the bright
use them as a means to take flight
take in the bad and turn it into good
and see the world in ways I never once could
with every breath, find new strength and grace
and see beauty in each and every face

Sacred

written in landscapes and skylines
is the value of life I soon will call mine
endured the whips of life
let go of the trauma of this enduring strife
a step forward taken with caution
rough exterior begins to soften
a heart once soaked from a downpour of tears
begin to dry them after all of these years
laid a heart on the line too many times
when the love I've always known is all mine
embrace the imperfections
smile at myself in all reflections
this soul has finally found its home
with a life still so unknown
yet, it awaits patiently
for me to find and hold onto sacredly

Architect

preying on the expected downfall
daggered words cut to my bone's deep core
resilient and steadfast, I remain standing tall
resilience flows more than your wishes to fall

go ahead and whisper, I'll let you plot and scheme
your doubts are nothing but echoes in my dreams
I am the architect of my fate
mature enough not to take the bait

rip me dry of my flesh but crave more
and if you expect me to lay myself to rest
watch as these broken wings find the strength to soar

In a Dream

in a dream lay oceans afar
a sprint through salty sand
follow the light of the north star
run too fast and the islands you'll miss
luscious and grand
and the safety you dismiss
miles ahead lie a volcano of grand size
it's large and intriguing
a structure that reaches the skies
should've stuck with the island
stopping sooner granted what I need
but when you mistake more for necessity
you mistake the volcano as a means of clemency

Return to Chapter One

quiet night in a crowded club
an indistinct song plays as our shoulders rub
bashful blue eyes meet my gaze
playing memories of future days
these moments are the ones I've missed
frozen heart suddenly sun-kissed
burning through all my barriers
remember the universe love has carried
the cheaters who've left me bruised
the one I so selfishly used
the love I thought was mine for eternity
begin to drift away fearlessly
once again return to chapter one
with a new one to call mine
and I hope for once
I finally got it right this time

Every Little Misstep

at a concert, they play a song we once listened to
not sure if it means anything
but it sure does remind me of you
getting emotional as they sing the bridge
the same lyrics they belt
are the same things we once did
and as the concert ends in one final dance
I see you across the room
as we exchange one final glance
with glazed eyes, we both stare
connected to you here
and in my heart everywhere

Nightly Rendezvous

I've been here before in the cold of the night
where memories come back with a haunting might
the guilt and sadness begin creeping in
giving into a night of my own sin

emptiness, disgust, and shame
the realization I'm not playing their game
I don't want to be part of this nightly rendezvous
where love is never seen through

walk away from the fleeting desires
and hold out for something that inspires
something real and worth waiting for
the peace that comes only when a heart is at its core

choose self-love and self-respect
over a moment that I'll come to regret
find solace in my own company
until the one who's meant for me I'll see

Remain Red

unexpected excitement a quarter until eleven
the dreams realized in this newfound heaven
strangers quickly turn to friends
no stranger to knowing how this typically ends
put on my finest face
this opportunity is too good to waste
how could this be true
somehow, someway, it led to you
relate to the reissue of Taylor Swift's "Red"
simple smiles and laughs exchanged in bed
once a place of my darkest days
turns to core memories that stay
seven months of wishing for a friend
seven months of debating over a life-to-end
never knew when my time would come
until there remained a new start with them
almost a year and restless we remained
drunken nights and shirts stained
tears shed in countless bars
broken hearts and temporary scars
so much can change in a year
and though the friendship has reached its end
I'll remember the nights it was pure
I'll remember the nights when we remained red

Coiling Pt. II

would you know that I've become so much more
than the one who thought waking up was a chore
would you know I've moved on from a love
that I once talked of endlessly and held high above
would you know I'm more confident than before
lose thirty pounds and the world I can now explore
would you know I still have dark days
or would you ignore it with a tinted gaze
would you know it hurts more than anything
that the disillusionment you bring
are the nights I was left coiling

Clear

look how far we've gone
took a bit of time
but the shadows of the past finally dawned

the same man who once was mine
in front of me now
two fragile hearts finding a way to realign

not yearning for a future
when we've blossomed so far
break awkward silence in awkward humor

all this time and we've made it in the clear
when the world battered us to the ground
we finally made it here

Garden of Growing Up

how is there guilt in carrying on with life
my means outweigh what you have expected
bottle of wine leads to dancing with tears in my eyes
slurring a half-assed apology to those who don't care
saying, "It's ok, I'm not the plague"
probably should've stayed quiet
wake up and fear it will soon be misread

why am I still justifying a lost cause
seek approval from those who dismembered my
limbs
took my health as a weapon of their entertainment
confide in friends who don't know the reality
living in fear every second
social standing was never an ambition
until getting caught in the misfire of he said she said

now they tell me they never had a good feeling about
you
even after the fallout, I still defend the things you do
breathe in and exhale in the corner of my room
a sip taken from Minerva's ambrosia cup
just another thorn in the garden of growing up

Velvet

quivered lip with an infectious grin
if life is a game of chance
for the first time in my life,
understand what it feels like to win
almost slipped and said three words
if the moon chorales in crescent waves
this heart will soon slip
and those words will be heard

time is of the essence so patience it'll take
there's no finish line in a race
when the clock is going at my own pace
lips send assurance and radiate velvet
the thoughts that continue to surge
and emotions never once felt

endless conversations until the clock strikes three
it's unraveling all at once
the best sides never imagined to again see
trembling to surrender this fragile heart
when the endless smiles finally give in
why wait for a moment to start?
when in this moment now you've claimed my entire
heart

24 Hours

across the stage with a wink and smile
heart stood still for a second
to fall in that instant was a life worthwhile

concocted in a whim and all eyes on him
how did the misunderstood
find the perfect set of eyes to look at me from within

when a reputation remains in such limbo
somehow look past all the cracks
instead of hearing of me, you get to know

set out on new adventures talking of my poetry
not sure if he truly understands
but for the first time, he's truly getting to know me

late-night crawls in a jazz-aged bar
it's been about 24 hours
but my god, the future I'm seeing spans so far

late at night and sprawled out on his sheets
looking down at me softly
with his subtly sincere brown eyes gazing back at me
this is 24 hours of feeling set free
cross my heart and hope to die
this is the right guy to have by my side

Surrender

four years of tribulations
of figuring out where I belong in my skin
surrender myself one more time
for a second, I truly believe this man is all mine
how did the universe place you perfectly into my life?
after time has shown love is an ongoing strife
but it feels safe here
it feels like I've found a home
a stranger a week ago
but my heart you fully have known

Lavender

a bitter end to a once-fabled life
battleground of my mind's strife
to once again reach rock bottom
amidst the middle of autumn
watch as the earth decays
my reality warping, turning sideways
winter awaits to chill the thoughts
of a heart tied into a hundred knots
in lavender-encrusted boots
I'll travel these roads to find my roots
see the skies as reminders of progress
the stars say, "Keep going, don't regress"
hold onto the mementos of my past
into a future that will forever last
with all there is left to see
it's time to return to me

Be Patient with Me

the crush of late December snow
how time has been patient with you
still waiting for you to give all you can show

how I've known you for so long
tease around hoping you'll leave
three months later, but you're still standing strong

sometimes I feel like you may be the one
I'm not ready right now
please be patient before you decide to run

if I let go of my heart once again
I want things to continue going slow
not have you as a lover first
but as a best friend

Wait for My Heart to Decide

gentle with my heart and patient with my moods
nobody's ever treated me like this
used to the eye rolls and quick attitudes

could go hours talking to you about my favorite
things
somehow you like them all the same
and did I ever tell you how much happiness that
brings?

I'm confused and worried
I'm alone, but assuring
won't give away my heart on more time
until I catch the moment
my heart decides that you're all mine

To My Grandparents

department store clothes and a toy train
toddlers enduring the struggles of growing pains
questionable cooking, but it feels like home
this vintage house is the one in which I've grown
catch the flu and a family runs ill
sledding down a slope in winter's chill
easter mornings with egg hunts ensue
Christmas gatherings and mornings of sudoku
illustrations placed on splintered walls
days at the park and the local mall
get news my grandmother passed
brushed it off then, but that pain forever lasts
soft echoes to the dog saying, "The babies are here"
but babies grow up, and the family dog disappears

can time slow down for my grandparents, please
the thought of them going is the thought I can't put
to ease
it's everything I am, everything I've become
without these traditions, I fear the memories will be
undone
hold onto these moments before they escape
for they remain the ones nothing else could ever
replace

Will the World Still Turn?

pushed away those on whom I could depend
I guess I never was much of a good friend
for all the cocktail-concocted altercations
it's me to blame for the tried tribulations
it's hard being alone in your room
when stars shed, I fear it'll soon become my tomb
it's nearing midnight and I walk around town
keeping my head down dreading you'll be around
below thirty as rain rushes into my skin
and God, do I regret who I have been
don't even feel like me, at least not yet
I'm human like you too, not an ongoing threat

thought I fell in love and was left ghosted
jumped the gun and too soon was I to have boasted
thought I was trudging down the right track
maybe it's too late to take it all back
thought my life finally had a meaning
maybe it's not even worth my time redeeming

twenty-two years of age and still learning
there's more to life than constant yearning
taking time to align my mind with my mouth
thinking, "Would the world still turn without me,
even if it's me you're now living without".

Cursory Connections

I could sit here and write this love was tragic
but when moonlight illuminates bent blinds
I remember the little moments of magic

so quickly young kids thought they found it
took a year to let my heart lead the way
it wasn't the wrong direction, though I hate to admit

the factors that storm within my eyes
keep asking, "Why did you have to leave so soon"?
was it your intention, or a short-run disguise?

in love's loss remains segments of anger
but this remains different
the highs of the time are ones I cannot find to tamper

draw the bow and find which emotions to target
embarrassment, confusion, or hurt
this earth stands still without you in my orbit

told you as it ended, "Please don't become a stranger"
even though intuition rang true
our cursory connection will never turn you into a
danger

Rewind

where is the boy who clung to his father's arms?
it's cold outside and I just want to go home
when it's past midnight who's to testify my harms
learn to live without loneliness, but to live alone

the boy at fifteen who salivated over validation
the men's gaze and the friend's care
yearned for the title of an association
but I would now tell that boy to beware
there's more to life than the acquittal
find what you're passionate about
others around you aren't always there to belittle
you need to learn what to live without
learn to live without love
learn to love without attention
learn to live from above
learn to forge your creation

that child who wished for the world
he's coming home to his mother's warmth
on a couch, tears streaming, and arms curled
telling me, "It's time for you to reform"
away from the illusions of my dreams
back to where it began
back to where I could once call myself
me.

Three-of-a-Kind

a year of latching to a temporary home
tides change and now watch astray
but wow, look how I've grown
the world once aligned amidst the middle of May

watch as I set free established friendships
was always told, "You deserve better"
even when the words were from an ex's lips
and the mindset encrusted on an old love letter
but he'd be proud I'm finally taking his tips

the girl met through work
the boy met on a dating app
the boy who is a walking quirk
the value of what's in front of me
are the friendships I'll keep sturdy

High Tide

the tide is resorting as the moon grows higher
actions of my words have become dire
rebuilding with broken bricks
striking a fire with singed sticks
it's coming back to me
even as those once sacred flee
find a new path to traverse
without those who hold my words to coerce
a history that cannot be revered

Repair the Rope

once weighed down by the dark clouds of life
I couldn't see a way out of the strife
but with each passing day, I fought my way through
and now I stand proud with life starting anew

two years have passed, and I've come so far
my depression no longer holds me in its shackling bar
I've conquered my fears and learned to be strong
and I'm grateful for the journey, though it's been long

I can do things now I never thought I could
with a newfound sense of purpose, I've understood
life is a gift to be cherished each day
and I'm proud of myself for finding my way

as I reflect on this journey so far
I'm grateful for the struggles, the highs, and the scars
for they've made me who I am today
and I'm proud of who I am
in every single way

Not the Same

one year goes by since my life forever shifted
a few hours of tears end in one final dance
my whole life I believed I could hold the clouds
but this life isn't wrapped in endless chances

no shame in the decision that was made
I was naive and you were headstrong
the silence that followed allowed our hearts to
cascade
the memories of our love are now distant and gone

in the darkness, I still see a flicker of light
but this time it's hopeful even during the hours of the
night
in every ending, a new beginning awaits
a chance to rewrite the tales of our fates
even when it'll never quite be the same

588 Days

close my eyes hard enough
and I can still remember your touch
the pieces that once were intuition
are fleeting at what condition?

the smell of detergent left on an old hoodie
the love is gone now, but always imagine what could
be
each day wrecks as I forget portions of your face
the one my hands could frequently embrace

the lap that could perfectly fit your head
should've captured it, but I always thought two steps
ahead
guess this is what's expected when mercury is in
retrograde
but sometimes I forget I once prayed for you to stay

it's fleeting all away
regardless of whether my mind has a say
it's all fleeting away
even after all but 588 long days

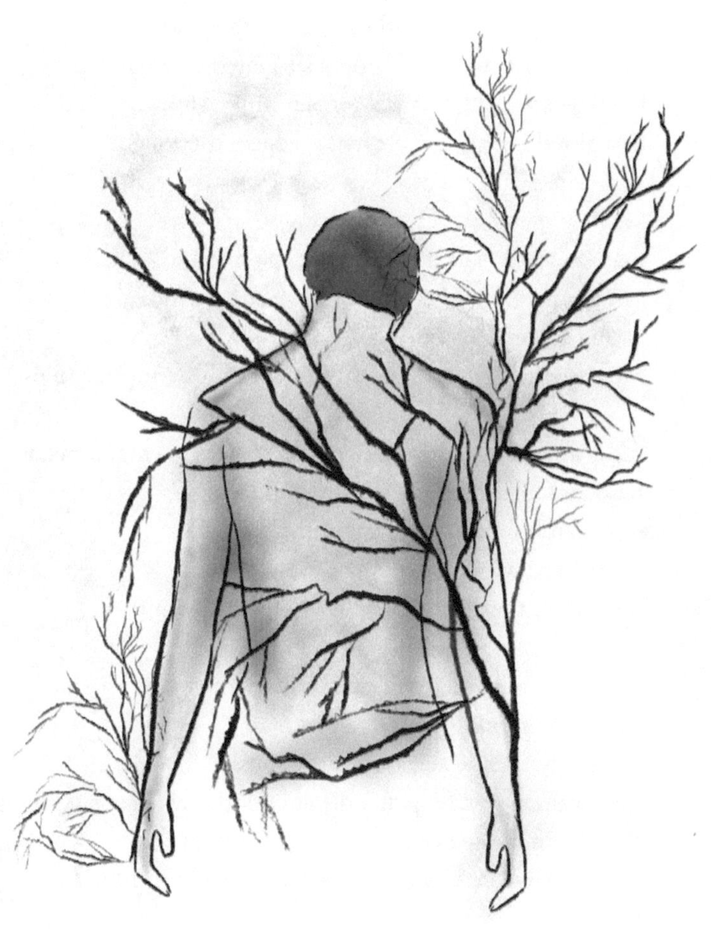

Borderline

when the dust settles over vintage stained photos
hope happiness is found away from the pain
alongside the nights of shouts and intoxicated ghosts
the ride was wild, but will remain my swan song
bad blood is only toxic when it lingers too long

see new memories created without me there
that glow that was missing once again found
assume I roll my eyes, but in my heart, I truly care
letting go remains one of wars and trials
my peace was found, and your faces returned with smiles

life is about making a step to give the world what it needs
hard and heartfelt, but beautiful and serene
it was an honor having you in this life
short-lived with quality times
but damn, these memories will remain all mine

I've been doing better if you wish to know
found my footing, found my ground
and my authentic self I can now show
I'll continue watching at a distance with my heart held tight
for the first time in months, I'm happy for you
that somewhere along the borderline we both found our
light

Weathered Boots

what I've known
since I've grown
and what I hold
are the words left untold
but I'll keep it with me
what we used to be
with all the memories

when the moon reaches its high
I'll grasp onto the sky
capture the memories of when you were mine
hold the stars forever the same
who you've made me forever ingrained
and I'm sure I'll see you out somewhere
in the winter amongst the solar flare
in the snow with weathered boots
if you brush past and don't give a second glance
just know
this harmonious tree will always remember its roots

End Goal

of all the actions I regret
memories ingrained I'll never forget
return to the life I once wished away
those who once believed begin to stray
accountability is only seen as gold
if the change created I can uphold
among this nostalgic silence is resilience
to push forth into a life of brilliance
evolving as the sun rises each morning
dark thoughts that emerge, just a simple warning
refuse to succumb to the doubt
and traverse down the incorrect route
refuse to forget the fight worth facing
the light ahead I continue chasing

grateful for what I had and what was in front of me
found love, true friends, and reconnected with my
family
rooting for the person I can soon be
and this time, it's a guarantee
symbiosis of heart and soul
feel it coming to patch the hole
though it was the trust I carelessly stole
going to get it right this time
for I finally found my end goal

Summer Symphony

in the golden haze of summer's embrace
the silence of campus becomes my cherished space
these days of my carefree youth soon shall cease
hold onto the little moments before they soon release

each moment is a souvenir I'll hold tight
for this summer is my last before life takes flight
through laughter and tears, I'll create memories grand
embracing the beauty of life hand in hand

during dusk, I'll venture under a starlit sky
venturing forth with spirits high
down dimly lit streets I'll explore and roam
these paths are the ones I'll always call home

around a bonfire, I'll share secrets untold
heartfelt conversations that never grow old
the crackling flames dance to the rhythm of our souls
bathing us in warmth as the night gently unfolds

morning coffee talks in nature's glow
sharing dreams and aspirations as the world starts to grow
as we venture forth into the realm of the unknown
I'll carry these memories forever on my own
though my friends may scatter, and our paths must diverge
I pray this final summer's magic will forever surge

Dissertation of Escapism

sinking slowly in ruins of cemented sweat
sun blinds dry eyes with gentle lies
cars pass into lives of monotony drowned by
amplified stereos
birds frolic in decayed dirt with naivety
and to fly with the birds is where a young boy wishes
to be
silently holding his breath for blue to turn black
when clouds shift to stars are when the voices attack
and god, this bed will never know a cold pillow
as the weight of the past continues to singe satin
sheets
in windows remain lives of false substance and
sentiment
while his consists of nostalgic nights on repeat
was the past as grandiose as the trinkets of his
remembrance?
hold the child who forever wished for the future and
lamented the past
he didn't know then, he still may not comprehend
he's going to turn out just fine
once he makes it to his end

PART IV
THE SYMBIOSIS

Intro to Symbiosis

a heart and soul aligned at last
found peace with demons of the past
no longer torn between life's many parts
embrace them all with an open heart
friends and family, both old and new
found my footing to see me through
as I learn to love myself
find the strength to heal and delve
into the depths of all I am
to find the truth that's everything grand
finding the light within my soul
let it shine and take control
for in the end, it's all the same
friends, family, and my own name
all parts of life that I hold dear
now aligned, and make my purpose clear
symbiosis of heart and soul
it's time to finally hit the goal

Symbiosis of Heart & Soul

grass-stained shorts
eyes reflecting quartz
indistinct laughter
rain passes for light to arrive after
sunburnt skin
a new love to lift my chin
a new friend to calm my soul
what once was broken, now becomes whole
a discussion with my heart
it says, "This is your new start"

forgive the past, let go of the pain
nothing will ever be the same
a symbiosis of heart and soul
lifelong journey, but finally hit the goal
within this life remains so much beauty
knowing I finally found a life that's worthy

This is Love

a shy laugh followed by brushing my hair
touch my hand in the twin-size bed we share
hold me tight and get lost in a soft stare

the moon is singing at this moment now
hearts cave in as we raise a single brow
not sure where you came from, but lucky you were
found

this is love told in effervescent beauty
this is love that belongs to me
this is love how I've always wished it be
this is love that has finally set me free

Cryptic Crossroads

lost a few friends and gained a new lover
to turn a new leaf is to find what to discover
cryptic crossroads of uncertainty
wherever it takes, I'll traverse purposefully
what's the purpose of redeeming my past
when I discern the light shown to forever last
people who don't cross-examine
each word that's left within
take my strides as counterfeit
for the mistakes I attempted to omit
my heart I've found in the graves of judgment
so why should I stand reluctant?

tackle the obstacles with a steady head
the road of ruin I refuse to tread
and if forgiveness is never granted
then forgiveness will never be demanded
capture the moments in which you shine
maybe few and far between, but it's a sign
for in this life, each decision you make is a decision
you choose
and in this life, I choose the road
in which my heart will no longer lose

Memories Traced

I used to think that friendships would last forever
we'd outlast the lows, no matter the weather
but life has a way of changing, and people grow apart
to find peace is to let go with a heavy heart

it's not that I don't care, or that don't want to be there
but sometimes, it's better to say goodbye to show I
care
it's not easy to let go of the memories we've made
the laughter and the tears are moments that won't
fade

for growth to take place
we must find our own path to embrace a new pace
though we may be apart, we'll always have a place
in each other's hearts with the memories traced

Wishing Well

the ocean will remain bountiful in its offerings
skip a few stones
where they land, will remain following
twenty-two years of age and still growing
love is not an anecdote of mastery
but one that encases itself in learning
hold a healing heart with each circadian beat
hoping once again
a soulmate is out there to finally meet

The Boy with the Guitar

the melodies you once privately shared
become songs that the world is now aware
getting the weight off your chest
of how an innocent love turned west

sing of reminiscing, regret, and pain
the love, the betrayal, and all the shame
dry eyes fog while hearing
but anger never considered when reliving is what's
left fearing

to find comfort in strained stories revolving around
me
hold my heart as I hear of the man I used to be
through the harmonies of heat-struck passion
on this ride with a seatbelt fastened

hearing you now through the static of stereo
seeing all the places you're bound to go
and you'll always be my boy with the guitar
with new expeditions set to take you far
recollect the memories with each replay
a year is so long to play a game of keep-away
when the life we once led will never once stray

The Best Sides

looking back on old memories
of a love that used to be
filled with happiness and glee
for the love that set me free

the laughter, the joy, and the tears we shared
all the moments endless with love and care
now become a distant memory of a love so rare
yet grateful to at once have you there

looking back with fondness and pride
hoping you find a new love that thrives
one that fills your heart with joy and light
shows you love that's pure and bright

to my lover boy who used to be
the moments we shared
are the moments that set my heart free
and whatever may be of your future
I wish you love that is pure and true
a love that brings out the best sides of you

Euphoric Dreams

it gets ominous past the hours of eight
shadows creep and fears begin to escalate
stare at my reflection and give a slight nod
I'm worth more than the rumors of being a fraud

you've been here before, so don't wait
cast off the doubts before the insecurities invade
tomorrow, show the world something to applaud
something that'll leave even yourself awed

these demons I refuse to once again infest
no longer a prisoner to their relentless quest
grown and matured too much to reminisce
deep breath in and suddenly feel bliss

close my eyes and lay this soul down to rest
not a man of good fortune, but feeling blessed
pray for euphoric dreams and well wishes
awaken renewed from the night's abysses

Strength of a Father

my father is a pillar of strength
love and guidance that goes a great length
though it's not always been easy to see
you accept me for whom I wish to be
through all the struggles and strife
taught me how to continue this life

showing me what it means to be a man
to stand up tall and take a stand
to be kind and caring, but strong and true
to tackle this life and follow through

and though we may not always agree
you've shown me what it means to be free
to be true to myself and never give in
to be proud of who I am and where I've been

Eyes of a Mother

to see the world from the eyes of a mother
is to see the world like no other
she who sets her heart aside
to patch the holes in mine
she who sees the beauty within myself
with gentle reminders of memories tucked in shelves
a gentle approach with a strong belief
I can be anything beyond my past grief
a future particularly paved by her past
endless sacrifices and love unsurpassed
no support like the touch of her hand
and to now see the world from the eyes of my mother
I now believe, I now know
to love a child is to love them seeing them grow
into all they were meant to show

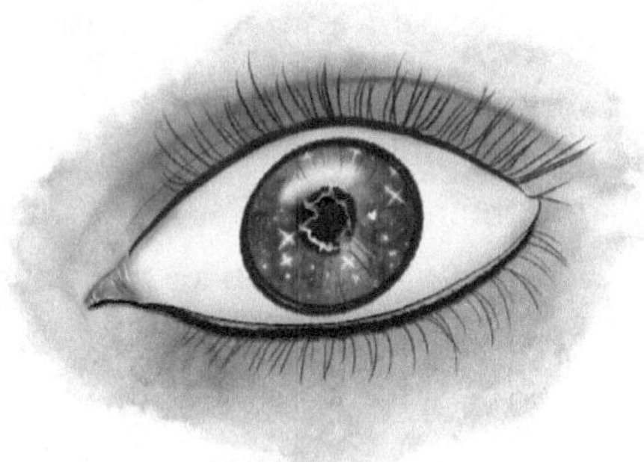

Happy New Year

January slipped like the ice on scenic byways
held my breath as the new year began
make a few resolutions wishing for brighter days
not yet healed, but this time I had a plan

whirlwind unraveled as my life changed forever
new friends, new experiences, new hope
slowly falling after each endeavor
drifted away and fell down a defiant slope

summer subsided along with the nights of highs
busted knees and disoriented dancing
ingrained memories that belong to me
it's gone now, yet I remain advancing

let go of all that once was to live as my own
I regret methodically, but not that decision
hold onto what's eternal and prove I've grown
a pessimist turned enthusiast after the division

found love through my friends and family
found love through my strides and strength
finding myself in all I can humanly be
I found myself within the span of a year
I found the lake in which I once stored each tear
I found what it means to finally be free

Ex Deposition

brazen beauties swarm nostalgic minds at nightfall
a shimmer of stars and faces of the past enthrall
the heart's pulse remains love's sacred memories
an ancient artifact of tarnished tapestries
love letters left shredded in a closet
photographs lose the gloss of their composite

sometimes the sun reflects images of each prominent
place
the same ones we once danced until dawn became
daybreak
when the weather shows signs of decaying
reminded of the nights of each bed once laid in
sharing secrets during the darkness of dusk
countless faces that once garnered all my trust

to regret love's impact is to regret how it transformed
me
invigorated spirit with a drive to be free
an isolated soul with a passionate heart
but to love is to find new ways to fall apart
a bearer of life's most sentimental side
finding ever-changing ways to guide
a crossroad in all one's life can find to divide

Little Things

new routines rise in rain-washed sediment
cup of coffee in a city vast and desolate
occupy the space between the ceiling and sheets
rise and walk around somber streets
scroll social media and get lost in the time
another youth was taken for an unspeakable crime
squirrels and birds sit at the front door
chewing on rotten fruit and coming back for more
a sprinkle of afternoon mist
is just an excuse to listen to Taylor Swift
a life that only appeared in vacant visions
stood in front all along waiting for my decision
arise each day in this methodical routine
another day of living my dream
a life of the little things
being the ones that are most serene

Colors Pt. III

may the landscapes of the forest decide
the colors waiting to be described
what once was painted in love
remain in mountainsides far above
hues that once were blurred
discovered as my heart unfurled
undertones saturated now with open eyes
witness the arrangements of earth's skies

melodramatic mornings shine of bellowing blue
clouds opaque with resilience as they pass through
evenings now effervescent in stark navy
stars sing melodies as they come to save me
the shadow of my own, once violet in an aura
transforming each day into its very own aurora

the colors I once could not describe
the colors I thought were lost
are the pigments of what's been missing inside
so long glazed over, but no longer glossed
the colors of myself a rainbow of change
each one absorbed as they remain in range
the colors of life now belong to me
the colors of liberation
the colors of what it means to be free

Hibiscus

I'm a hibiscus flower blooming bright and bold
my petals finally shine with burnished gold
forever a symbol of love, passion, and grace
an eccentric beauty with a fragile face

had to bud to blossom, but unfurled with ease
these new vibrant colors are a sight to please
a reminder of life's cynical nature
there must be growth and renewal
to achieve a bright future

so when you see a hibiscus in bloom
remember my message and dispel the gloom
embrace each moment and live without fear
blossom and flourish year after year

Compass of Campus

coffee talks with the mirror
three teaspoons of sugar
slow sips to counteract the future growing nearer

one foot out in crisp winter air
snow caresses university pavements
sends shivers through perfectly placed hair

gaze upon buildings cloaked in glitter
it's coming to an end soon
the memories garnered I hope don't bitter

friends earned, lost, and held with me
parties raged, forgotten, and regretted
but there's no place I'd rather be

made a home within the compass of this campus
the same one I first fell in love
within the lake that still shines of lapis

each aspect of this life has led me here
the beauty and pain all my destiny
to grow into an individual where life I no longer fear

Gabbie

in a haze of wonderstruck confusion
if friends are life's core
forever find ways to keep them losing

painted and proclaimed as a villain in these streets
but when rumors run ramped
it's your eyes that mine forever meets

shine a light on the best sides of me
teach me to forgive the past
live not in nostalgia, but as it should be

late night outings lead to early coffee talks
drank a few too many shots
just another night of endless highs distorted with
broken clocks

in all life's games, you always have a part of me
the same part that knew you were special when I was
twenty
for there would be no life worth living
without my best friend, without Gabbie

Wyatt

during the summer I met a boy from thin air
looks of gold that made others stare
everyone wants him, that's clear to see
jealousy never considered, just happy he found his
way to me

met him for his heart and quickly became my friend
distance endured, and still, he remained at the end
a heart that's pure with a soul that's just as aligned
finding a friend like this is once in a lifetime

listens when I need a willing ear
when boy problems arise, I'm there to hear
there for me through thick and thin
when the world felt like a constant losing game
he was the only one who made me believe I could win
stripped away once, but found your way back
with you in this life
I feel like I can continue coursing down the right
track

Chris

last-second decision led me to a bustling club
fate played its game as I discovered a new form of
love
so quickly you met me for my soul
the façade I portrayed you quickly stole
others mocked, just the misguided few
but I knew in my heart I had loyalty to you
severed the ties and left my friends behind
for the sake of something that was for once genuine
and kind
since then you have taught me how to be
daily porch parties where our hearts ran free
sips of wine as we laughed and cheered
sharing stories, and just happy to have you near
picnics at the park as the sun hits our face
creating memories time cannot erase
slumber parties while celebrating pride
one year later, and still, you remain by my side
days at the pool with impromptu photoshoots
didn't mean much to you, but felt myself return to my
roots
and as the stars shine and cast their vibrant glow
just thankful to have someone who will never go
never thought a friend like you I could find
my darling,
I think I'm going to love you for a long time

Tethered Threads

what once was soft and new is now tethered and torn
the blanket with frayed threads where memories were
born
22 years grown, and still by my side
the one thing in which I could always confide

laughter and tears and always holding me close
these tethered threads are the home that only I know
it's beginning to fray, and its colors slowly fade
but it's comfort is one thing that has never betrayed

in the darkest of nights, it was my only light
a steadfast presence when I almost took my life
witnessing heartaches and triumphs and the days of
feeling blue
and a constant reminder of the lovers I once knew

for in each stitch, a story now resides
of the blanket that's been the one thing consistent
through all of life's tides

Tapestry of Life

in the tapestry of life, friendships intertwine
a once vibrant connection now fading with time
cherish the moments shared in the past
laughter and long talks, a bond that will last

though our paths now diverge, and bridges have been burnt
I hold no resentment and I no longer yearn
for my heart wants a future for you that's true
happiness encasing in all that you do

though you still mock and bring me down
won't let the noise make me drown
for there is beauty behind this temporary façade
will learn to love from afar, even when what you do remains
hard

in the depth of my soul, I'll find a way to prevail
release myself from you and watch as my heart exhales
I want you to find joy, success, and be content
even if we're no longer part of one another's ascent

hoping maybe one day I'll show what I've become
grown wings of strength beneath the setting sun
if that day never dawns, I'm at peace with the thought
that our memories together were lessons taught

the tapestry of life weaves intricate threads
a symphony of moments where our story spreads
parting ways remains one of gratitude and grace
having this friendship that left an undeniable trace

Fruits of Forgiveness

there remains such serenity in a step forward
small in stature, but strong in fortune
seasons shift as does the mind of myself
let go and cling to all life brings in portions
serenade the world with what's found left

this is beauty told in the mind of mistakes
not indebted to redeem a future
when accepting what occurred in the past
defines more of who you were
and where you are headed

take in the highs of each souvenir within life
it's a core aspect of forging an identity
take the missteps as a ladder to climb
soon the haze will fade to obscurity
for there's a light if you believe

the fruits of forgiveness will be handed in time
take ahold of what's currently mine
away from the flocks and crowds
into the grace of open skies and luscious clouds
another sleep, another day
reminding myself that everything will be okay

First Fall of Snow

as the first fall of snow crests barren roads
I remember the valuable lessons my family once told
each day an opportunity to seize
before the life we lead one day belongs to god's skies and
nature's trees
hold onto what's facing your direction now
let your heart guide what once was if you allow
the Christmas memories of those who are now gone
coloring books from Grandma and the old family dog
as each year continues to pass by
continue forward with reminders of why
I must never take the importance of family for granted
for their love is what's eternally implanted
savor each moment, year, and Christmas
before time slips by and misses us

hold onto each record bestowed by my grandfather
meant the world as I'll carry them in his honor

continue to store each birthday card left by my mother
never say it enough, but forever I love her

carry the jerseys of my childhood which remind me of my
father
leave them for my kids to one day discover

store the texts sent late at night from a worried sister
read them later at night when the gloom arises mid-winter

the small mementos that remind me of home
are the memories I'll continue to carry on
a piece of my family wherever I go
the piece of my heart I'll never outgrow

Pages of the Past

the words upon the past pages
of the books I've long since read
are more than simple phrases
or talks that once were said
they hold within their covers
a glimpse of who I've been
the joy, the tears, the lovers
and all that I've seen

"the universe he carried"
escaped me to distant lands
showed in heartbreak we can be married
to the stars and shifting sands

"heartbreak and healing"
an anecdote used to soothe my soul
finding love again was more than a feeling
and a broken heart could once again grow whole

"half a life / half a lie"
was a mirror of my past
helped to untie
the baggage that held me fast

"losing grip" was a recent warning
to catch hold on to what I love dear
taught me life can be soaring

but just as quickly disappear

these books have shaped my being
they've helped me transcend
they've taught me about feeling
and how to make amends
these past pages
have shaped who I've become
all of the wisdom, pain, and fun
all of these words are what I have left to show
and have led me to this day
where uncertainty finally finds a home

A Brother's Love

my sister forever my guiding light
through life's ups and downs, she's held tight
love unwavering and sacrifices grand
a true friend forever with an outstretched hand

through thick and thin, she's been there
a constant source of love and care
she's given up so much of herself
to help her brother improve his health

she who has seen him at his best and worst
and loved him still no matter the cost
together weathering life's storms
and come out stronger in each other's arms

my sister has sacrificed it all
for her brother who can now stand tall
a bond so pure and real
the greatest gift of all
a bond that the world will never be able to steal

Where Hope is Fed

in life I too often make mistakes
carry them closely with a heavy weight
regrets that linger deep within
haunting me like an unshakable sin

but there comes a time to let it go
and release myself from the pain I know
forgive myself for all that's passed
and embrace the future and be free at last

for in forgiveness, I found strength
to move beyond and go to great lengths
to grow, learn, and make amends
to chart a new course, and make new friends

with each step forward I've gained new ground
confidence building in leaps and bounds
becoming the person I've always meant to be
strong, resilient, bold, and free

no longer holding on to past mistakes
time to let go and give myself the breaks
forgive the past and look ahead
to a brighter future
where hope is fed

The Life I Choose

haven't gone out much these days
"He's out with another boy," they say
and for once the rumors are true
basking in the water of my youth
not much remaining, but it's the life I choose

living for the thrill of the unexpected
bright lights and blaring music
this is living at 18 even at 22
embracing the colors of my existence in every hue
not much remaining, but it's the life I choose

dancing through nights without regret
each moment a memory I won't forget
the laughter, the love, the fleeting views
not much remaining, but it's the life I choose

with friends who feel like family
in a world that's ours so candidly
we chase the dawn and refuse to lose
not much remaining, but it's the life I choose

for in this vibrant and reckless spree
I find the truest part of me
living each day as if it's brand new
not much remaining, but it's the life I choose

Reclaimed

will a sun-soaked soul warm a cold heart?
grasp the grass as I let the healing start
count each and every bird
hear their chirps, understanding each word
once burdened by so much trauma
placed in one too many dramas
silence is so serene
when the past can't intervene
get lost in a maze of my mind
and for once let the thoughts be kind
look at how far I've come this year
took my time, but I'm finally here
my body is no longer a shame
my past no longer bringing pain
who I am is not the same
and in this healing
my soul I have now reclaimed

Eclipsed

delights of dangerous tomorrows
subside along the past of saturated sorrows
never neglected the sun to shine brighter
when my friends instilled I'm a fighter
when the rain was a reminder of my past
I'd once line up buckets and follow the forecast
a new age with awakened senses
burnt down bridges to amend new fences
grasp onto the goodness I once carried
set free the pain that I've too long buried
and when the sun and moon align
the eclipse of heart and soul finally became mine
a symbiosis of sacrifices and salvation
for a world that's awaiting my every creation

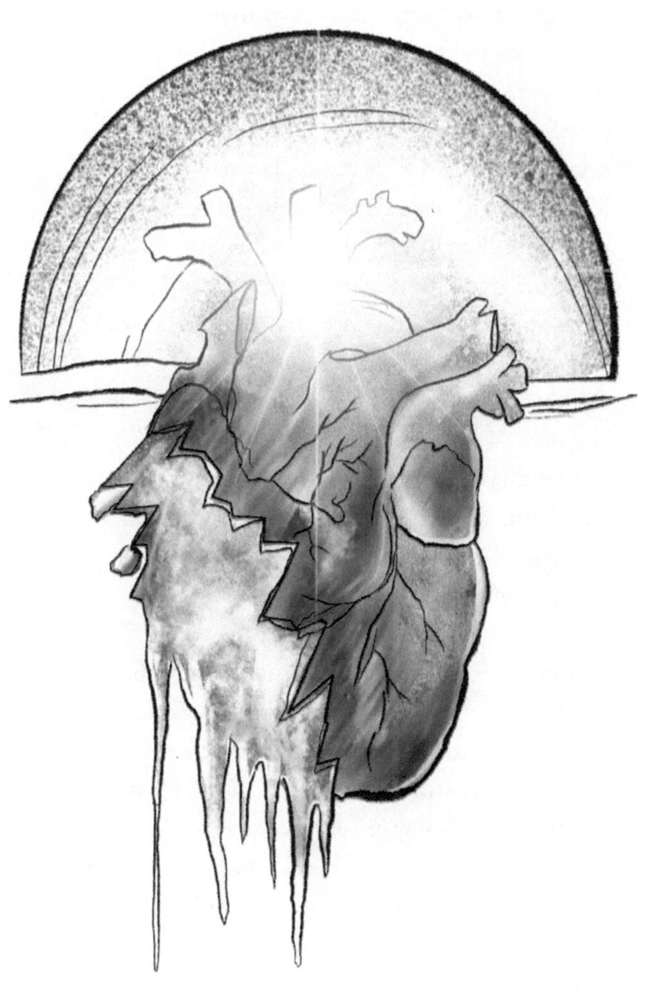

The Universe I Carried

this heart now beats at a regular rhythm
away from the thoughts of him
two years gone, and I can breathe
sapphire of skies I once again see
grieving subsided to focus on living
long talks with friends and nights of forgiving
memories may flash within dreams
wake up, but happier than I've ever been
faces appeared in fractions, but I'm now ready
foot on the gas, this time no longer going steady
flash past the memories that once belonged to me
the sights I experience I can clearly see
the healing that came from heartbreak
the shame of living half a lie
the night I had to let love go
remain souvenirs that you'll only truly know
the past becomes a glimpse of a life you've only viewed
this new adventure one of grandiose gratitude
the symbiosis has arrived to grant what I deserve
peace, love, and a life I can confidently serve
my place on earth becomes one of the fourth dimension
the body bag I prayed for has gained an extension
let go of love, let go of friends, and found my value
doesn't revolve around others, doesn't revolve in navy blue
revolves around the body blessed to me
and with symbiosis of heart and soul, I now know…
this is exactly where I'm meant to be

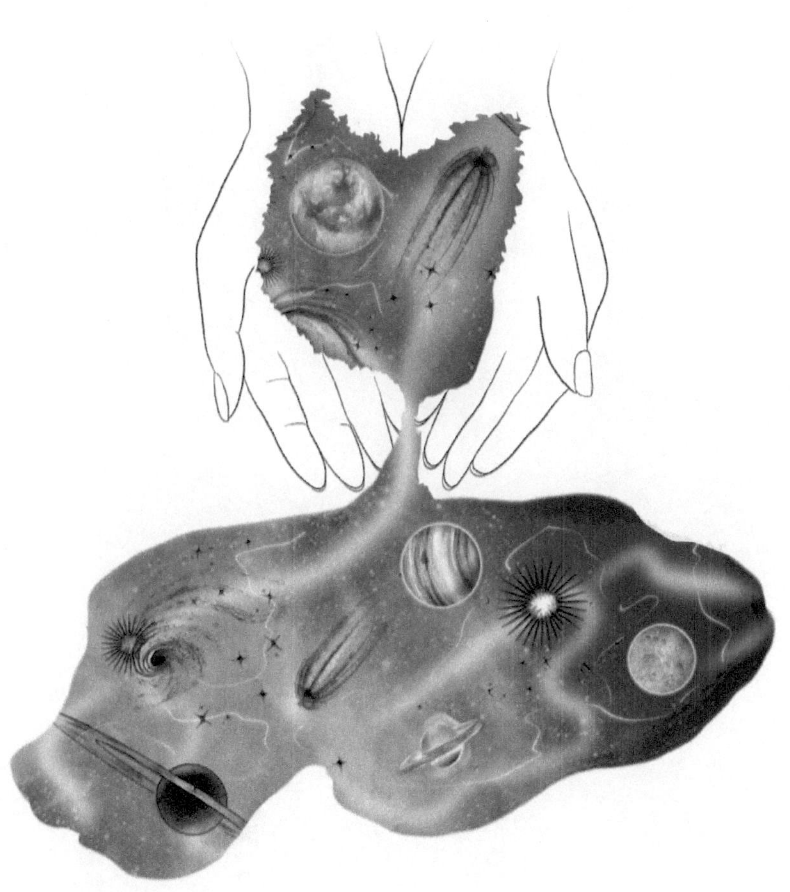